GEMS
NATURE'S JEWELS
AQUAMARINE

By Tayler Cole

Gareth Stevens
PUBLISHING

Please visit our website, www.garethstevens.com. For a free color catalog of all our high-quality books, call toll free 1-800-542-2595 or fax 1-877-542-2596.

Library of Congress Cataloging-in-Publication Data

Cole, Tayler, author.
Aquamarine / Tayler Cole.
    pages cm. — (Gems : nature's jewels)
ISBN 978-1-4824-2860-5 (pbk.)
ISBN 978-1-4824-2861-2 (6 pack)
ISBN 978-1-4824-2862-9 (library binding)
1. Precious stones—Juvenile literature. 2. Gems—Juvenile literature. I. Title. II. Series: Gems, nature's jewels.

QE392.2.C65 2016
553.8'7—dc23

2015006323

First Edition

Published in 2016 by
Gareth Stevens Publishing
111 East 14th Street, Suite 349
New York, NY 10003

Copyright © 2016 Gareth Stevens Publishing

Designer: Andrea Davison-Bartolotta
Editor: Kristen Rajczak

Photo credits: Cover, p. 1 Nadezda Boltaca/Shutterstock.com; p. 5 Nastya22/Shutterstock.com; p. 7 Associated Press/ AP Images; p. 8 Vegnus/iStock/Thinkstock; p. 9 Joel Arem/Getty Images; p. 11 (top) T photography/Shutterstock.com; p. 11 (bottom left) Fribus Mara/Shutterstock.com; p. 11 (bottom right) J. Palys/Shutterstock.com; p. 13 (main) De Agostini/G. Dagli Orti/Getty Images; p. 13 (inset) S_E/Shutterstock.com; p. 15 Patrizio Martorana/Shutterstock.com; p. 17 creativepro/Shutterstock.com; p. 18 Mauro Cateb/Wikimedia Commons; p. 19 Brendan Smialowski/Getty Images; p. 20 Rob Lavinsky/iRocks.com/Wikimedia Commons; p. 21 tarras79/iStock/Thinkstock.

Printed in the United States of America

CPSIA compliance information: Batch #CS15GS: For further information contact Gareth Stevens, New York, New York at 1-800-542-2595.

Contents

Words in the glossary appear in **bold** type the first time they are used in the text.

What Are Aquamarines?

Aquamarines are blue or blue-green **gems**. They have great **clarity** and a glass-like luster. "Luster" is the glow created when light shines off something. Aquamarine is a very hard gemstone, which makes it perfect for making **jewelry**.

Aquamarine is the most common form of a **mineral** called beryl. The gem's color comes from traces of iron within the beryl, which is often colorless. Aquamarine's name is connected to its beautiful color. It comes from Latin words meaning "seawater."

Be a Gem Genius!

Another well-known gem is a type of beryl—the emerald!

4

This beautiful gem is aquamarine.

Historical Gemstone

Aquamarine has been used as a gemstone dating back thousands of years. Ancient Egyptians and Hebrews valued it greatly. Greek sailors wore the stone when they went to sea to please the sea god.

Today, the leading producer of aquamarine is Brazil. India, Russia, and Madagascar are other major sources. Aquamarine has been **mined** on Mount Antero in the Colorado Rockies since the 1880s. It's found thousands of feet up the mountain in the highest gem field in the United States.

Be a Gem Genius!

In 2004, an aquamarine crystal measuring 37 inches by 25 inches (94 cm by 64 cm) was found on Mount Antero.

These aquamarine and diamond jewels once belonged to Grand Dutchess Elizabeth Feodorovna of Russia.

7

Creating Aquamarine

Beryl crystals form within igneous rock, which is created when hot, liquid rock from deep within Earth cools. Aquamarines are often found in a kind of igneous rock called granite pegmatite.

The color of beryl crystals depends on the minerals present in them. That means aquamarine crystals can be found right next to other gemstones! The most famous types of beryl are aquamarine and emerald, but others include morganite (pink), heliodor (yellow), and goshenite (white).

liquid rock

Look at all the different colors of beryl!

What Does an Aquamarine Look Like?

Aquamarine gemstones don't come in many different colors. They're always blue or blue green. Some blues are lighter, and these are the most wanted for jewelry. The aquamarines worth the most money are the deep, dark blue stones. They're **rare** in large sizes.

Aquamarines are often treated with heat for a long time to make dark or low-quality stones look more blue and less green or yellow. The stone can't be heated at too high a temperature, though, or it will become discolored.

Be a Gem Genius!

The best aquamarines are transparent, or able to be seen through.

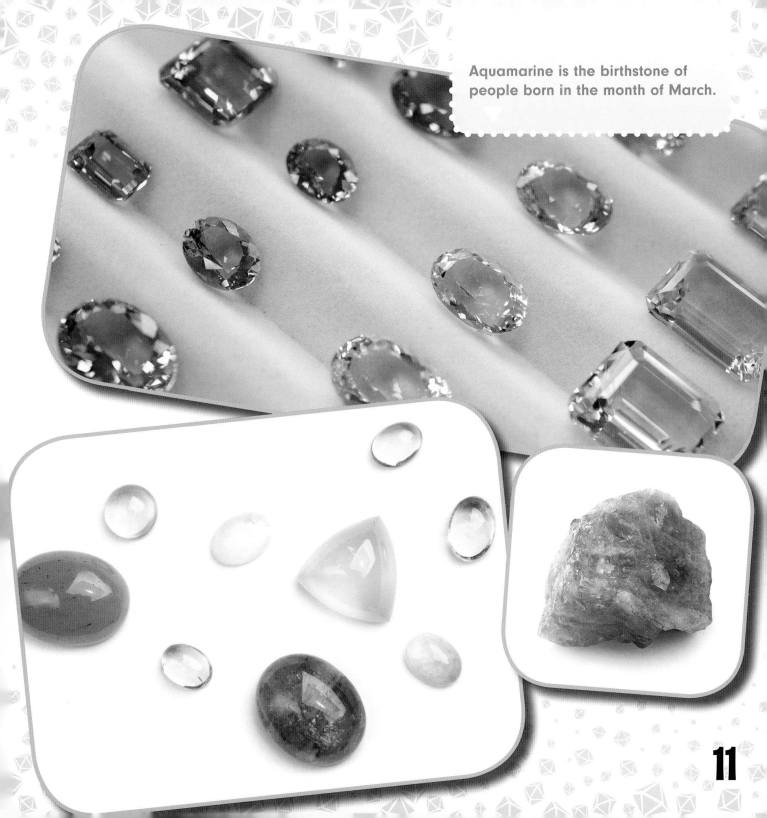

Aquamarine is the birthstone of people born in the month of March.

Finding the Gemstone

Like many gemstones, much of the aquamarine people see comes from a mine. Once a **vein** of aquamarine is found, miners break up the rock into smaller pieces. They then use tools to dig out pieces of aquamarine. After aquamarine is free from the rock where it formed, the gem is carefully washed with water.

Mines aren't the only places to find aquamarines. Sometimes, a person hunting gems just for fun will find aquamarine in a place it's never been found before!

Be a Gem Genius!

People looking for gems like aquamarine or for gold and silver are called prospectors.

Minas Gerais, Brazil, has many gemstone mines, including aquamarine mines.

Everything About Aquamarine

All minerals have certain qualities they're **classified** by. Beryls all have a glassy, or vitreous, luster and a hardness that's between 7.5 and 8 out of 10 on the Mohs scale of mineral hardness.

Aquamarine crystals are hexagonal, or six sided. And though they're hard, they can break, or fracture! When they break, beryls have a smooth curve at the point of fracture. Aquamarine and other beryls are brittle, which means that when hammered, they'll become powder or small crumbs.

Be a Gem Genius!

Luster, hardness, and fracture are three of the main qualities mineralogists look for in minerals. Tenacity, or how a mineral reacts to being crushed, is another.

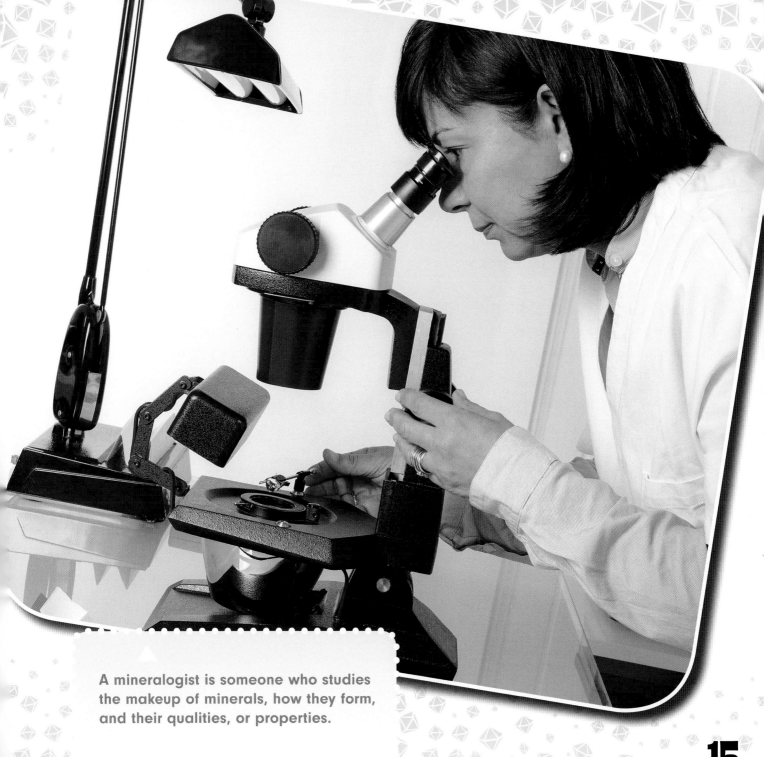

A mineralogist is someone who studies the makeup of minerals, how they form, and their qualities, or properties.

Making Aquamarine Jewelry

Before being set in a necklace or ring, an aquamarine has to be cut and **polished**. Often, these gems are cut into a rectangle or square with many sides called facets. A cabochon is a gem cut into a circle or oval with a rounded top and flat bottom.

Sometimes small pieces of different minerals inside an aquamarine create cool effects! The minerals **refract** light into the shape of a cat's eye or a star. Gems with the star effect are worth a lot of money.

Be a Gem Genius!

Aquamarine may also be cut into small figures. These are often made from opaque aquamarine, or gems that aren't transparent and clear.

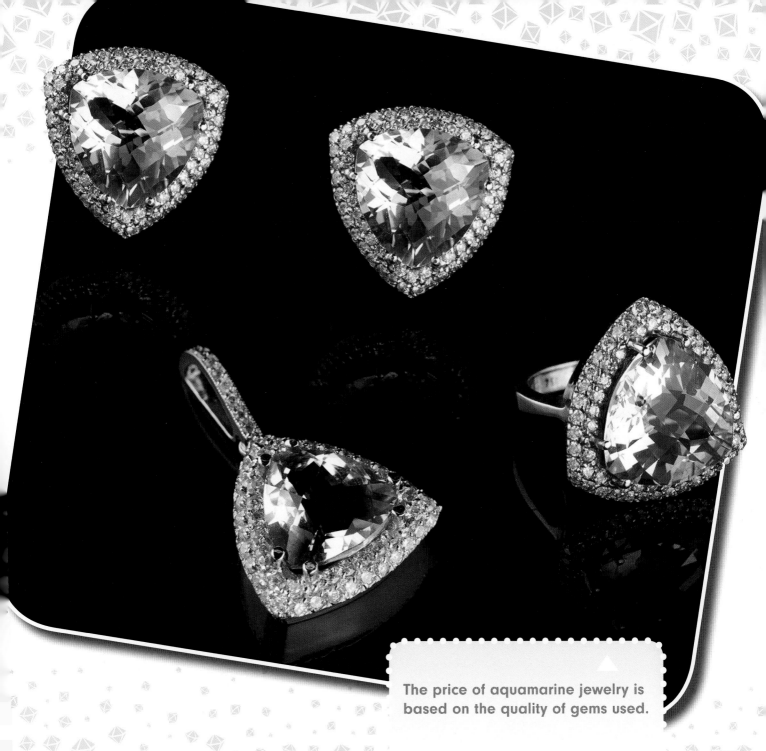

The price of aquamarine jewelry is based on the quality of gems used.

Really Rare Aquamarines!

In 1910, an aquamarine stone weighing 244 pounds (111 kg) was found in Minas Gerais, Brazil, an area known for aquamarine. Called the Papamel aquamarine, the stone added up to more than 550,000 **carats**! It was nearly perfect, too.

The largest faceted aquamarine is the Dom Pedro aquamarine. It's about 14 inches (36 cm) tall and 4 inches (10 cm) wide. It was mined in Brazil, but today it's at the Smithsonian National Museum of Natural History in Washington, DC!

Often when large stones of aquamarine are found, they don't have a high enough quality to be cut. The Dom Pedro is an exception!

Powerful Aquamarine

Tales have been told about aquamarine for centuries. It's said to have special powers, including keeping sailors safe and stopping seasickness. Sick people would place the stone upon the ill or hurt part of the body because aquamarine was believed to heal, too.

These are just stories. What's certain is that aquamarine is a beautiful gem that people have valued for a very long time. As more and more aquamarine is found around the world, that's sure to continue!

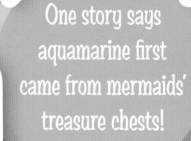

Be a Gem Genius!

One story says aquamarine first came from mermaids' treasure chests!

Find Aquamarine!

Aquamarine can be found all over the world, including in the US states of Maine, New Hampshire, Connecticut, North Carolina, and Colorado.

Glossary

carat: a unit used to weigh gems. Five carats is equal to 1 gram (0.035 oz).

clarity: clearness, the state of allowing one to see through

classify: to assign something to a category or class based on shared qualities

gem: stones that are cut and polished and worth money

jewelry: pieces of metal, often holding gems, worn on the body

mine: to take rocks and other matter from a pit or tunnel. Also, the pit or tunnel itself.

mineral: matter in the ground that forms rocks

polish: to make smooth and shiny

rare: uncommon or special

refract: to make light change direction

vein: a narrow channel in rock

For More Information

Books

Lawrence, Ellen. *How Do People Use Rocks?* New York, NY: Bearport Publishing, 2015.

Morgan, Ben. *Rock & Fossil Hunter.* New York, NY: DK Publishing, 2015.

Symes, R. F. *Eyewitness Rocks & Minerals.* New York, NY: DK Publishing, 2014.

Websites

Aquamarine
gemkids.gia.edu/gem/aquamarine
Read more about aquamarine, and see cool pictures of this gem.

Encyclopedia for Kids: Gemstone
encyclopedia.kids.net.au/page/ge/Gemstone
Learn all about different kinds of gems.

Index